The Soul Goal

Lance T. Painter

To Kenni,
yo! yo! yo!
love,
[signature]

LANCE T. PAINTER

Thank you to Linda Gadbois
of Colorado Springs, Colorado
for the beautiful cover art for my book.

Copyright © 2013 Lance T. Painter

All rights reserved.
ISBN-10: 1479328944
ISBN-13: 978-1479328949

LANCE T. PAINTER

FROM THE AUTHOR

Looking at my personal library and my reading habits, I realized that I have always been attracted to small books. To me, they are to the point with impactful content that inspires me. I have read books that captured my interest in the first few paragraphs making me eager to continue reading the remainder of the book. I then am able to experience a shift of consciousness or a psychic change by studying and repeatedly re-reading certain books for years. How often do we read a book, have an awesome awakening and feel inspired when we're through, only to then put the book away? My goal here is to be to the point and not be verbose. While writing this book I felt as though I was a vessel. I put the pen to the paper and the thoughts and ideas began to flow. My primary purpose and hope is that I can pass my story on and inspire other lives to love no matter what his or her past has been.

FORWARD

I felt validated and encouraged by this story, knowing that another person with a similar background to mine has also come to the same conclusions. We each choose the path we take, some mindfully and some not, I chose love despite my turbulent past. Love comes in many forms but the greatest love is healthy self-love. Lance's words made clear that if we don't have a healthy, unconditional love/respect for ourselves we don't have a chance at having a truly wonderful relationship with another human being whether it be a friendship or a romantic partnership. Those of us who did not have a "perfect" childhood need to be reminded not to allow ourselves to get stuck in the past - but to flow forward, no matter how slow the progress. If we can improve someone's life through our positive behavior we have truly moved mountains.

Not too long ago I overheard a man I know who has a doctoral degree, and is well into his thirties, who remained emotionally distressed about certain aspects of his rearing. I had an impulse to speak to him about considering looking at the situation from the perspective of his parents. Then it hit me that until he has made a conscience choice to want to heal and move past this hurt it didn't matter what anyone said, his inner being would not accept reason. The fog will never lift until one makes a simple choice that they want to progress though this maze we call life. Once an individual makes that simple decision it is amazing how new ideas appear. Unfortunately, when someone grows up in fear it can take some time to allow the voice of our heart and soul to be heard.

Thank you Lance for writing a book that teaches and often just reminds us of what we subconsciously already know. This book is for the enlightened person, but mostly for the person who wants to be enlightened. Our thoughts create our own limitations and our thoughts can create our freedom. Opening our minds seems like a difficult prospect but it can be as simple as saying to yourself *yes I want to let go and allow new ideas to flow in* as they will. Not all new ideas will be helpful, but all should be considered: what excites me, what has true meaning for me, what makes me feel joy. Think on these things.

The illustration on page 35 was very therapeutic for me, in my case I sometimes need a reminder to not allow the fog to return as it can and will if we are not mindful of and using good cleansing techniques presented; then I got your title of the two foot drop. If we approach our life with the tools in the heart as you suggest we will be on our way to a future that is going to be fulfilling, purposeful and bring satisfaction.

The exercises in chapter 6 are simple and truly can assist the honest person in realizing self-awareness. Often realizing our ownership in a negative situation is hard to look at, but necessary if we want to progress. It is a hard truth to realize when we accept the truth that we have chosen at some level to be in the situation we are in that is causing us discomfort. Encouraging the reader to physically write out what is wanted can bring joy to replace the feelings caused by the first assignment.

This book is truly filled with nuggets of wisdom and well worth several reads.

Again, Thanks for sharing.

Sincerely,
Leslie J. Shouse, LPN
BA in Education

LANCE T. PAINTER

CONTENTS

From the Author	v
Forward	vii
Acknowledgments	xv
Preface	Pg 1
Chapter 1 WHAT HAPPENED? A Soul Sickness	Pg 5
In essence I had become the person who created my wounds	Pg 8
I was still having fun and partying but my perceptions of life began to shift	Pg 10
Choices, relationships	Pg 10
Little Brother Where Did You Go	Pg 12
Mom and Dad – Fatal Attraction	Pg 13
My life as a child and adolescent left me thinking that I was responsible for the emotions and feelings of those people close to me	Pg 15
Chapter 2 WHAT IS FEAR? Lack of Information + Lack of Self Love = Ego FEAR: The Grand Illusion The Filling of Empty Space	Pg 17
The power to create and the wisdom to know the difference	Pg 22
All of us have the choice and the ability to find it within ourselves	Pg 24
Chapter 3 DOUBT – THE SET UP How We Allow Bad Experiences To Put Us In Limitation	Pg 25
The Head and the Heart	Pg 26
Your own life is the "present." Unwrap the gift of "you"	Pg 28
Doubt – Sabotage, the enemy attacks	Pg 28

Doubt leads to fear, leads to judgment, leads to execution	Pg 29
What is real, is unreal – and – What is unreal, is real	Pg 29
Shattering the Illusion	Pg 30

Chapter 4
WHAT'S LOVE GOT TO DO WITH IT? EVERYTHING — Pg 31
Self-Esteem + Self-Awareness = Self-Love

Love is ultimately everything for which we are searching	Pg 32
Self-awareness – the greatest loving thought and decision we could ever have is to decide to embark on a loving relationship with ourselves therefore giving us the ability to truly love others	Pg 33
Diagram of the head and the heart	Pg 35

Chapter 5
THE HEAD WE CHOOSE TO LIVE IN AND THE HEART WE LEFT BEHIND — Pg 37

I am absolutely certain that I chose this life, all of it.	Pg 39
The Epiphany	Pg 41

Chapter 6
UNCOVER, DISCOVER AND RECOVER
"When We Are At The Edge Of The Cliff The View Is So Clear" — Pg 45

When did we become the executioner of our dreams, our happy ending, and most importantly how did we become jaded?	Pg 45
Who? What? How?	Pg 47
My part	Pg 48
Sample self-help tool for Self-awareness	Pg 50
Sample chart for personal relationships	Pg 51
The Law of Attraction	Pg 54
The new dream, love and happiness	Pg 55

Fear and the law of attraction, Pick a Dream	Pg 56
Purpose of Amends	Pg 57
A New Life Awaits You	Pg 58

Chapter 7
RELATIONSHIPS/CHOICES
"You're the smallest brightest light in the center of it all, as it unfolds, as it should. You can wait or you can choose to begin." Pg 59

Be smart with the heart	Pg 60
Codependency	Pg 61
Individuality	Pg 62
A look at the four elements of a successful relationship	Pg 64
Table diagram	Pg 65
*Communication	Pg 65
*Honesty and Trust	Pg 66
*Respect	Pg 68
*Listening	Pg 70
Intimacy In-to-me-I-see	Pg 71
Continuity Continuing – unity	Pg 72

Chapter 8
YOU: The Final Chapter, Forgiveness Pg 75

Glossary of Words/Feelings Pg 77

ACKNOWLEDGMENTS

To all of you I am truly grateful and I thank you. I love you all so much. The people throughout my life that have given me enough care and regard to tell me the truth – I thank you. Also to the people that have taken the time to care enough and to be honest with me, as awkward as I have made it for them to be that person – I thank you. I am grateful for the integrity and conviction in these people that have truly made all the difference in my life. These have been my true friends.

I would also like to give acknowledgement to all my children, Courtney 27, Joshua 18, and Christian 17. These are my beautiful, precious gifts from God, innocent and vulnerable, wanting to know and believe. They are my opportunity to teach them the wisdom to know the difference, between right and wrong, and fear and love. They have given me the opportunity to give back what I did not have in my life.

To Trudy for showing me what REAL authentic love is.

LANCE T. PAINTER

PREFACE

My original title of this book *'Good News I Found The Other 90%'* was a play on words derived from the scientific idea that we only use 10% of our brain capacity. My perception is that quite possibly 10% is the full capacity of our brains while the remaining 90% is our heart, soul, divine inspiration and intuitive thoughts and feelings that give more clarity in guidance and decision making.

I think it is true that some of us are only using a fraction of that 10%. This vision or perception became clear to me a couple of years back after spending the last twenty plus years seeking balance, truth and understanding in my life. You see, I came from a severely dysfunctional family and a world filled with many mixed messages.

In the early stages of developing the concept of this book, for some reason a train became the allegory that I envisioned to thoroughly understand what i wanted to convey to my readers. Let's look at a train. Say the engine pulling the train is the brain, or the 10%. If the engine is not fully up to that 10% or does not have a good mechanic maintaining it, a sudden left could cause it to jump the track taking the remaining other 90% with it. That train, big enough and going fast enough, if derailed, could take out a whole town. Truly a crazy train! When applied, this scenario can offer a stark example of how detrimental decisions made solely on our 10% of knowledge can be.

We all have a heart - a good 90% somewhere. We all want love whether we consciously know it or not. This concept for some can seem to be deeply embedded in the woods. Still others may see it clearly at the edge of the forest just waiting for them to take hold. True understanding of it depends solely on how open a mind the individual possesses.

For some of us our 90% is fully functional and we need to focus on our 10%. This 10% we can label as choices, discretions and decisions. While some of us have done well with our 10% as far as choices go, we still are lacking a true connection and application of that remaining 90%. Either way there is hope because at any time we can uncover, discover and recover. Taking the time to step back and no longer live in confusion, doubt and fear. We can become a fully functioning love train. How many people live and die without experiencing a truly healthy and loving relationship?

It is what awaits you. It has been said that success is nothing without someone you love to share it with. That someone could quite possibly be you. We are all worth the time it takes to step back and get to truly know ourselves and love ourselves unconditionally. We are all worthy of a peaceful, loving and understanding existence. My challenge to you comes with encouragement to begin the journey today of seeking the greatest love story ever told...... *Yours*. We can manifest the successful relationships we want to have in this lifetime, because if we can see it, if we can feel it, then we can be it, so....pick a dream.

Lance T. Painter

LANCE T. PAINTER

CHAPTER 1

WHAT HAPPENED? - A Soul Sickness

I grew up in Los Angeles, California in the 1960's. I fondly remember the sparkle of it all, sunshine, the ocean, entertainment and good music on the AM radio. The "Real Don Steele" was a famous DJ on the radio at that time for those of you who may remember. Born in 1961, I would venture to say the radio must have been playing in the delivery room as I entered the world because I latched on to music right from the start and created a great kinship with it. Throughout my life I have called music my religion. My family life was anything but conventional. For starters, my mom liked to party and never was able to overcome her addiction to alcohol. In fact it was alcoholism that eventually led to her death at 58 years old, a relatively early age by today's standards. My father shared the same love of drinking as my mom. He also had a wandering eye, which led him to leave my mom when I was about 4 years old. He would continue to pop back in my life for a day or two at a time, but there never really was any substance to those visits. I viewed him as the funny man who would make us laugh and then disappear again. Through it all it was music that kept my heart alive. Even today it gives me inspiration as I listen to Marvin Gaye while I am writing this.

My turbulent upbringing resulted in me being seasoned (I like to say) in codependency at a young age. It was unavoidable for me with my loving heart and the constant desire for things to be better. The shining light of love and togetherness has always been a beacon for me. As a kid my true heart's desire was for everybody to love each other and get along. It was music that led me to find my theme for life, and confirmed what I'd always considered my driving force – Love. I received that message from the man I have always viewed as a prophet, John Lennon. His message 'All you need is love' made perfect sense to me.

My mind was filled with doubt, confusion and fear. In our family, I was the middle child of three. My younger brother, Tayo, came into the world on Halloween in 1969. My other brother is 14 months older than me. About one year before my younger brother was born my mom's drinking spiraled out of control. It was so off the charts that my mother could not handle us both and sent my older brother to live with our grandmother. Tayo was born a year later and for the first 2 years of his life I was his dad and mom all wrapped up in a brotherly package. I was 8 years old. At 10 years old Tayo and I were separated and each placed in foster homes. It was a sad time for me, as I loved him very much. In my heart he was my 'little cubby bear'. I loved him so much that at the age of 11, I made it my goal to take care of him the moment I turned 18. Although the idea was love based, it was quite a remarkable, if not admirable goal for an 11 year old boy. This was the beginning of my confusion between the head and the heart. This was also the beginning of doubt and fear taking hold of me.

I was in eight different foster homes from the time I was 11 until I was 16. Later in life I realized that for my mom, her attempts to better her situation and take time for herself to get herself together resulted in an inconsistent home life for me. Putting me in foster homes only further represented her continued failures at bettering herself. By the time I reached the age of 14 my mother had taken me in and out of the group homes so much that my social worker made me a ward of the court to try and stop it. But, the "system" is what it is and I continued to be moved in and out of three more group homes until I was 16 years old. By then my mom had a new man in her life that seemed stable and owned a home in the San Fernando Valley. This apparent stable home led my social worker to release me from being a ward of the court and back into my mom's care. It was not long until I realized her new man was a good, stable, functioning alcoholic. I soon dropped out of high school and gained a new found freedom. After all those years of acting like an adult, worrying about my mom, brothers and myself, it was apparently time for me to be a kid (hindsight). I found drugs, friends, and rock and roll. It was soon after finding this freedom that I begged my stepfather to teach me how to drive a '73 Ford Pinto stick shift. The very night I learned to drive it, I rolled it down the driveway and went and picked up my friends and WOOHOO! I was off! The selfish regard for me and my needs and desires had begun. I was finally going to do what I wanted, when I wanted, and for as long as I wanted. I realize now I totally bottomed out at 19, but even so I was years away from realizing what the bottom really was. *In essence, I had become the person who created my wounds.*

At 19 years old, I was somewhat of a nomad, living out of my 1967 Ford Econoline van and parking outside my mom's apartment building so I could grab a shower each morning. About midnight one evening, totally motionless and completely sober, I felt alone, and completely empty.

As I lay in that van I felt no real meaning to my existence. Up to that point, my life had been full of empty relationships. It was at that moment the song started playing on my van's stereo *'Da da da da de de de de de de da da da daaa, love, love, love, da da da da, love, love, love...'* and the words from John Lennon pierced my soul like nothing ever before. 'All you need is love, it's easy...' That is the night the seed was planted. That was the night I found something to search for and obtain.

I was a "rebel without a clue."

After this awakening, I resolved to change my thoughts from negative to positive. I remember starting to change my thoughts to positive by simply thinking positive thoughts. I thought positive thoughts constantly and for a while things did begin to change in my life. I got a job and that job brought more positive people into my life. ***I was still having fun and partying, but my perceptions of life had begun to shift.*** When I was 24 years old I met and fell in love with (or so I thought) the woman who would become the mother of my first child. Because I was receiving love from her I figured the obvious next step in this (my first real relationship) was to slow down and settle into home life. The truth is that at 24 years old there was no way I was equipped to give love or receive love. This is where the work began.

Choices, relationships

Without being fully equipped with the facts about ourselves or any essence of what is true for success, we are a train wreck waiting to happen. At that point in my life, a relationship to me was best described as *'since she loves me, this is meant to be'*, and lacking the tools I needed to make the right choices, I led my life using the trial and error method as my guide. Having never been loved unconditionally in my life, I took her love for me to mean because she loved me I owed my life to her. In short I was clueless. It was this that led me right into detox in 1989 at Dana Point, California when I was 28. It was in those prior 4 years, from the time I was 24 until I was 28 years old, I was able to see clearly the bottom and the problem which led me to begin digging for answers and looking for solutions. Recovery had truly begun. For me, without total abstinence from drugs and alcohol there really could be no starting point of truth.

My first step was the process of eliminating the fog that drugs and alcohol created for me so that I could clearly define my problems. As being an admitted alcoholic/addict in recovery today, I believe that drinking and drugging is but only a symptom of the problem. The problem was Lance. I didn't have a clue about any tools and I certainly didn't know how to have a truly happy life. A closer inspection of my life at that point would have revealed repeated actions mirroring those of someone who intended to commit suicide. I would use drugs for days on end without food or sleep only to bottom out *(die)* at the end of my binge. This was my way of life and I personally had to 'die' many times in order to finally 'get it'. Today I am grateful to be alive and able to tell my story and pass it on for others. Now it is with all of my being that I believe everything happens for a reason. The fog has lifted for me and I am living my purpose today by writing my story. If my experiences, hopeful findings and solutions bring clarity and hope to just one other life by reading my book, I am truly serving my purpose and none of this was in vain.

'Little brother where'd you go?
It was just like yesterday we were playing draw
You went your way, I went mine
Little brother I've come to believe where you've gone
You had enough pain and confusion and you were blessed
Now you're soaring with the best
My little brother, my little friend, I'll see you in the end.'

These lyrics I wrote when my brother died.

I had been in recovery for about a year when my little brother, Tayo *(my little cubby bear)*, who was 20 years old, was shot in the back and killed. At that time, my mom and I were both in recovery. Tayo's story was a sad one. He was in and out of *"the system"* from the time he was 2 years old until my mom and I found him at a boy's ranch when he was 16. As a result of his tumultuous life, he was plagued with many problems. My mom got custody of him and tried to deal with his problems, but being newly sober and trying to make a lifetime of amends, this was overwhelming for her. As the story goes she never really was equipped with the tools to follow through and overcome these obstacles.

I was uncovering, discovering and recovering myself at this time and sharing a good relationship with my mother. Both sober and finding a new fellowship between us, I found my entrepreneurial spirit and started my own business. For about 3 years my mom and I had a loving, available and communicative relationship.

Mom and Dad ~~Fatal Attraction

'It was in the San Fernando Valley during those three years when one day, as we were driving in the car a song began to play on the radio. I looked at my mom and she was smiling so lovingly, as if she was in a deep trance. I asked her, 'What are you thinking about?' She replied, 'that song (on the car stereo) reminds me of your father.' The song was 'Love Lift Us Up Where We Belong' by Joe Cocker.

It was not until I had married and moved to Arizona that my mom suddenly became unavailable by phone. I found out that the reason was because she took my father back into her life. After being separated and divorced all of my life, my parents thought that now they could have the relationship they always fantasized about. My mom had 5 years of sobriety and my Dad had been sober maybe a week, within 6 months they both were drinking together again. It was while my mom was in the hospital having surgery that my dad literally drank himself out of this world. I went to Los Angeles to bury him and get my mom out of the hospital. I got her situated the best I could and then headed back home with my wife and babies. Four months later she drank herself out of this world the same way as my dad. Curiously, she died in almost the exact spot as my dad had in their apartment. My mom now rests at Forest Lawn in Los Angeles with the headstone that reads, *'Love Lift Us Up Where We Belong.'*

Mom & Me: In loving memory of Joan Linda Quick

My first marriage lasted 8 years and resulted in two beautiful boys. Unfortunately, I had to ask for a divorce because I was very unhappy and I could not make her happy. As I mentioned before, I was seasoned in co-dependency at an early age. *My life as a child and adolescent left me thinking that I was responsible for the emotions and feelings of those people close to me.* The responsibility of caring for both my mother and brother in my childhood took its toll. Additionally, the relationship I had with my mother was one in which the parent/child roles were reversed. I became accustomed to always worrying about other people's whereabouts and well-being. I was trained very well and very early to think that this is what a healthy, loving relationship looked like.

In retrospect, I now realize that my mother's love for my father was the only love she knew in her lifetime. Even with 5 years of sobriety, my mom never had the experience of real love, or a successful relationship. She was unable to work past the fear and find the tools she needed and try to apply them. Her story is not unlike so many of us. Truth is, even then, I still did not possess those tools either. The good news is that today I am aware these tools exist for me and you alike. All that is required to obtain them is a mind open to growth and the desire and willingness to take some time off and look within. My search is what led me to the message of this book. No matter what, you can overcome all of the experiences you have had so far, find real love, and have successful relationships in your lifetime. *You can create, manifest, and CHOOSE to MAKE THIS HAPPEN!!!*

CHAPTER 2

WHAT IS FEAR?

~~~~~~

Lack of Information
<u>+ Lack of Self Love</u>
= Ego

~~~~~~

FEAR: The Grand Illusion
The Filling of Empty Space

Fear is an emotion, a feeling we get as a result of an experience or situation we had encountered. What we fear is not always a fact. At times, and with 100% of our being, we are positive it is a fact, although it is not. I would like to present you with the idea that of the thoughts we experience in our head, at least 90% are fears, and those we experience in our heart (our soul) are love. The head is fear. Likewise, the heart is love. There is a clear difference for me today between good, healthy decisions and fear based ones. We have all heard the phrase *"my head said no but my heart said yes."* I tend to believe this utterance comes out of the mouths of those who are not quite ready to accept ownership of their own growth. This may be a victim role, blaming the heart. This usually means they had a healthy fear or a healthy caution based on experience, but they did it anyway. Therefore, how often have we heard or said the statement "I have to stop listening to my heart." Confusing as that statement is we fear heart based decisions "blame vs. ownership."

I am not saying that fears are not real at times. I am simply breaking down what is real fear *(caution from experienced concern)*, and what is not. Most of us are unaware of just how much we have been limited by our fears and failed to reach and experience our true hearts desires in our life. I will share with you one of my first and best examples of this.

I grew up playing guitar and jamming or collaborating with other musicians. We would get into a jam session and occasionally have what we all considered a creative masterpiece. After that experience we would frantically look at each other and say, *"Do you remember how we did that? Wow! We should have recorded that"*. This helped me realize that I could change my thoughts and beliefs at any time. From these experiences I started to change my fearful thoughts that I would not remember what we played, to confident ones that next time we would be even better. Since then I have realized that all the music and writing is always inside me. It is always there without having to worry *(fear/hallucination)* that it will go away. This is just one example of the endless fears we have that limit our pure potential.

All fears originate from a single thought. How you feel or to what extent you are affected by fear depends on which level of fear you are having. For example, I have felt fear through my solar plexus, through my arms, through my legs *(Have your legs ever shaken out of fear?)* or through my stomach to the point of throwing up. If fear can do such powerful things through our body, imagine what damage this can do silently and internally in the long term. Essentially fear produces stress. Do you think it might be possible for us to have a choice in the matter and heal ourselves through different choices in our thoughts/fears?

I reiterate, most fears are not facts. I think most fears are best described as hallucinations. If we view them as such, how much do you think we hallucinate in one day? Do you attribute other people's success to luck? Maybe they have managed to obtain a better focus or maybe they're luckier than you because they had the opportunity to further their education and get a degree and you did not. Whatever your reason may be, I can assure you that good decision making can become your best attribute at any time, as long as you are open minded enough to learn. Luck has nothing to do with it at all. I am positive proof education or luck has nothing to do with this because I dropped out of the 10th grade and have never had any formal education since. I did not have any real consistent family, let alone a loving and supportive family, growing up.

Prior to 2009 I had been consistently self-employed for 9 years as a land developer and had some great successes and definitely some not so great experiences with my personal and professional relationship choices. Although I was still learning how to manifest through living without fear and was willing to experience the love I wanted by being willing to say YES, I got married for my second time. Struggling through 2008 to hang in there with my real estate career and my marriage, in early 2009 they both collapsed, and more was to be revealed.

For the next 3 years I had the opportunity for the rest of my illusions to be shattered. I had the opportunity to bottom out on all levels. I would like to put it as *"I put my sandals on and started walking."* Once again, I became a nomad. I had the opportunity to live in the *"I don't know."* I was willing to risk my comfort and security to go on a journey of *"I don't know"* and *"where do you want me to be God?"* This led me to move 24 times in a 3 year period.

Easter Sunday of 2009 I wrote affirmations on a yellow notepad of who I was and what I wanted. I will never forget how excited I was to share this with my wife at the time. As she read it she replied, "It must be nice to know what you want". This experience confirmed two people on different tracks. After all we had gone through in our two and a half years together; it was at that moment I realized we were strangers. Two weeks later, I moved out.

In May 2009, being 45 days late on my Chevy truck payment; it was repossessed by the finance company. Immediately, I reacted as I have my whole life, but this time something came over me to not fight – and to let it go. *I surrendered.* Three months later, I fell behind on the payments to the storage unit that contained all of my belongings. The storage company told me they were going to auction off the contents of my storage unit. I said ok. The best way I could describe this experience is- I would see something open up *(a place to live or a new job)* and say "I guess this is where you want me to be." If it didn't pan out, then I would simply say "OK," rather than react. Hindsight today is that I had to let go of reacting and the drama around me with my emotions to open myself up to anything, which is the experience of NOW, this moment.

Judgment and expectations on outcomes had to be shattered. Shatter the illusion. I proceeded to move and live in Sedona, Arizona for 1 year from September 2009 to September 2010. Sedona is a magical place that will surely help you process things on a fast track whether you like it or not. Sedona spelled backwards is anodes *(connections, according to the thesaurus)*...interesting. In short, my Sedona experience seems like a place a lot of people have gravitated to, to find themselves, while others are still searching. There are some truly divine masters that have found themselves in this enchanted place. Nonetheless, Sedona was, and continues to be, a magical experience for which I am grateful.

The power to create and the wisdom to know the difference.

I am no longer a victim and I never was. What I learned in

those 3 years, what I call my "stripping" on all levels, showed me the true meaning of acceptance. It showed me the true meaning of "I am" and "I am not things." It broke me of the habit of being a reactor, and taught me how to be a creator each given day of each given moment. The same letters are in both words, the difference is where the "c" is - *See ("c") where you want to be.*

It is true that some people had better loving influences than others, while some of us had to hit walls and figure it out, then lived to tell their story about it in books like this one. We all start out on the same playing field. The only limitation we have with our experiences come from within us. The freedom to take control of our thoughts and experiences comes from within us when we accept the fact that we are not, and never have been, victims at any time in our lives. I do not believe I am a victim nor have ever been. Quite the contrary, I know everything I experience comes from within me. If I reflect back on my life I could probably find that some decision in my past has led me to a problem I am having today. Knowing this was my motivation to include an exercise for you later on in this book. It is truly the best way to evaluate your life and see it clearly today. The goal here is to live with peace, freedom and acceptance, and to live in truth. I believe that there is only one truth. It is that truth that sets you free to be happy and joyous. Luck and education played no part in these things whatsoever in my case. I simply changed my thoughts and in the process I came up with the best line I've ever written to explain my success, *"For it is whatever we believe that we achieve...Pick a dream."* **All of us have the choice and the ability to find it within ourselves.** This concept of the balance of the head and the heart was strong in me the prior 5 years before writing this book. My hard experiences combined with a keen sense of divine intuitive direction are what nudged me to share my understanding of the balance between the head and heart with the rest of the world.

FEAR: **F**uck **E**verything **A**nd **R**un

-or- **F**ace **E**verything **A**nd **R**ecover?

The choice is yours.

CHAPTER 3

DOUBT – THE SET UP
~~~~~~
How We Allow Bad Experiences To Put Us In Limitation

I have already made reference to the two human motivators, love and fear. In the same category with fear is where we will find doubt. Doubt itself gives us plenty to talk about. Doubt, or I would say "a healthy concern", can be a good experience. However, doubt can stem purely from a lack of belief in Self also known as self-doubt. If your doubt stems from the latter, it is safe to assume we now are getting to an awakening and to self-growth.

Again, it is our beliefs that limit us. So, maybe the solution can be to expand our belief, create a bigger or better belief, which I would call growth or an awakening, leading to a greater awareness. I remember my own epiphany of how I could overcome doubt in my own life. It was some years ago when I was kicking around the idea of starting my own business. I was 31 and living in Los Angeles. One night I was lying in bed contemplating starting a windshield repair business. I was coming to terms with being a business owner. My mind kept running through the adventure of obtaining new accounts at car dealerships and trying to come up with the name of the business. *(Ultimately I named my business 'Crackbusters' - I fixed cracks in windshields.)* The moment it all clicked into place for me was paramount. *"I can have a business."* Then positive thinking took hold, *"Why not? Other people can and so can I."* This moment of clarity helped me overcome the doubt in myself I had in regard to my ability to become an entrepreneur. I forged ahead, got a business license and within 2 years I had secured 27 dealership accounts throughout the Los Angeles area.

The Head and the Heart

We are so hard on ourselves, doubting and judging ourselves. When toying with a new idea, quite frankly, doubt, fear and judgment will limit us to the point of paralysis. I like the word "judgementalist." We sometimes can be professional judgementalists. If we closely observe our thoughts we can identify which ones we want to extinguish, and in the process change ourselves through our thoughts *(the foggy, tainted mind of the human head/heart equation)*. Try for just one day to pay attention to your negative judgment of others, and especially of yourself. I am certain that with this self-observation you will be amazed at what goes on regularly in the human mind on a daily basis. I assure you, this is where the beginning awakening lies. Doubt and failure can be deeply rooted within us. Once we can fully identify what and how much is constantly going on, we can begin.

My thought exercises are always evolving, and currently, depending on how I am feeling or whom I might be judging, I stop myself and ask *"Is there any love in this?"*. I began thought changing exercises at the age of 19 when I spent about a month pursuing the obsession of saying all day long in my thoughts, *"think positive, positive, positive"*. Today I believe when I want to know what course to take, I just need to slow down enough and focus on my intuitive direction, the clearer, untainted heart/soul of the human head/heart equation. My experience is that if I do this, I will surely know what path to take. My personal perception of Jesus is that he was the coolest dude who ever walked the earth. He was all about love, happiness, abundance and true success within. I am not a religious guy. I am spiritual with a belief and respect for individuality, happiness and freedom of choice when it comes to personal choices like that of religion. God is Love and Love is God.

I believe the truth will set us free. The truth is love, and freedom is peace and serenity. The world I know, that we live in, is set up for doubt and fear but we all have a choice in it. I believe none of us are victims. I believe that everything happens for a reason. I also believe the reason is for strength, with experience and hope, leading to service of others. But we only obtain these things if we choose to look at it that way and stop playing the victim role or the blame game. I can see clearly today that all of my experiences are to serve a purpose, to serve with purpose. My goal is to help others with hope, courage and experience, which led to the knowledge that you can overcome anything if you open your mind and become willing to let go and surrender. **Your own life is the "present." Unwrap – the gift of "you."** Welcome to the "I don't know." No matter what your past has been, it truly is possible for all of us.

Doubt – Sabotage: The enemy attacks

Have you ever found yourself in a great experience, a truly out of this world relationship? Someone you just met and everything is so fun and synchronistic, a magical experience each day, having an absolute wondrous adventure together?

Then, all of a sudden, the energy shifts (reality sets in) – which I will explain is not reality, but perhaps on old dream, an old reality, a dream of limitation? A dream of "I knew it was too good to be true." Our self-judgment thoughts of "I am unrealistic" and "what was I thinking."

DOUBT LEADS TO FEAR, LEADS TO JUDGEMENT, LEADS TO EXECUTION

This is how we become our own executioner of our happy ending or happy beginning. We were literally flying together in a beautiful experience, blissful synchronicity, "in the moment." Then suddenly, we looked down and did not see the ground under our feet and got scared. I will say over and over in this book. "We are the creator of everything we experience."

What is real, is unreal – and - What is unreal, is real

There has been a dream that has been shaped and formed for years on this planet. We have been told mostly everything that has been unreal is real. For example, true love only happens in the movies. Television and films have given us a perception that we are separate. We pay good money to watch cable TV. We pay good money to go to the movies. We go mostly to experience, watch a dream other than our own, other than the one we are currently having. Now I am mostly talking about inspirational feel good movies and romantic films. Truth is, all of those films, books, and music were created by people just like you and me. We have the dream inside each of us. We have the creativity inside all of us, including YOU.

Shattering the Illusion

We are not separate. There is no "us" and "them." This simply is why you have seen such amazing works come from, what we call amazing, inspiring people with backgrounds of childhoods that had no influence of real healthy love, childhoods that were abusive and negative. How can they be such great beams of light? Why can't you?

CHAPTER 4

WHAT'S LOVE GOT TO DO WITH IT? EVERYTHING
~~~~~~
Self-Esteem + Self-Awareness = Self-Love

Love, it's what we all truly want whether or not we know it. Although the '60's summer of love really did change the world, I feel that it ultimately closed a lot of minds to the word "love" today. This was largely due to the lack of responsibility that was demonstrated by the heavy drug use at the time. It's funny how our associations become fixed. The idea was real – *all you need is love*. But bring something like that up today and, depending on who you are talking to, they will tune you out after making the assumption that you are a hippie on drugs. Fact is, love is such a foreign word in society today. Yet in reality, it is all that is real. Love is a substantial and tangible good feeling of inspiration.

Disaster of any kind gives us a great example of the reality of love. Why do you think it is that when a disaster happens, people pull together with unity and love? Remember, in the late '80's when Jessica McClure fell into the well? America as a whole was glued to the television until she was rescued. As a nation united we banded together, prayed as a whole, and felt the emotional upheaval of this experience right along with the entire McClure family until Jessica was thankfully rescued. It is important to acknowledge that just as we collectively hoped together, television or any media outlets can cause us to collectively "feel" and share any emotion they choose.

All of that aside, **love is ultimately everything for which we are searching.** How many of us go to a movie theater to see the perseverance, true love and the happy ending that we all personally want in our own lives? How many songs do we hear that pierce our soul, our heart and tie us into our true heart's desire whether we consciously know it or not? How many of us simply have just given up because of our past associations with love? How many of us are jaded and closed off with a fortress around our hearts? How many of us have not been jaded and still believe in love, but simply cannot understand why we cannot accomplish or manifest the relationship of our true heart's desire in this lifetime? These questions are the heart of this book. The work, clarity and truth lies within all of us if we are willing to slow down and spend a little time to look within. We can all experience true love from within.

We have the tendency to be propelled with our ego and self-will combined with our tainted information from previous life experiences. When we surrender and open up our foggy mind that drives us, we begin to hear our divine inspiration. Our personal intuitive direction that awaits all of us is called the heart-soul.

**Self-Awareness - The greatest loving thought and decision we could ever have is to decide to embark on a loving relationship with ourselves, therefore giving us the ability to truly love others.*

When you end a relationship with someone, is not the irony always that you thought you knew them or wanted to get to know them better? Is that not a process we should have figured out by now? My experience leads me to believe that it takes four to six months to begin to know someone. Of course, this is only if they know themselves. How about the experience of knowing the one you are in a relationship with more than they know themselves? WOW! Is that not awkward? The answer to relationship issues begins with a loving relationship with one's self. All of us are so worth taking time off and truly connecting with our *self*. We tend to be the person thought of last when it comes to love. After one or more failed relationships how many of us will take time off to reassess things? However long it takes will we take time to get a clear picture of what is going on, a clear picture of our choices? Self-awareness is compassion and understanding and the purest form of love - *Self-love*.

This morning, as I continue writing it is November 5, 2008. Current events have given me another example to add to this book. Last night, our nation united like never before and elected a man named Barack Obama as the next President of the United States of America. Barack Obama inspired us as a whole and ignited what lies within us as a nation. Collectively we experienced the love, hope and ability to believe that which we all have within. Last night I watched as thousands of people in Chicago gathered at Grant Park and even more lined the streets, all because they believed in the dream of hope, and together were motivated by the spirit - Love. It is there within all of us. "Inspiration is the food for life." To be inspired is love itself, and passion at its purest. All of us have it. It awaits our choice to find it and journey with it throughout our lives. The Doobie Brothers, *"Oh oh ooh, listen to the music"*. It is all around us, it is always inviting us and it always has been.

THE TWO FOOT DROP – SOUL GOAL

The real question is, "Are we listening"?

THE FOG: The Dream of the Planet

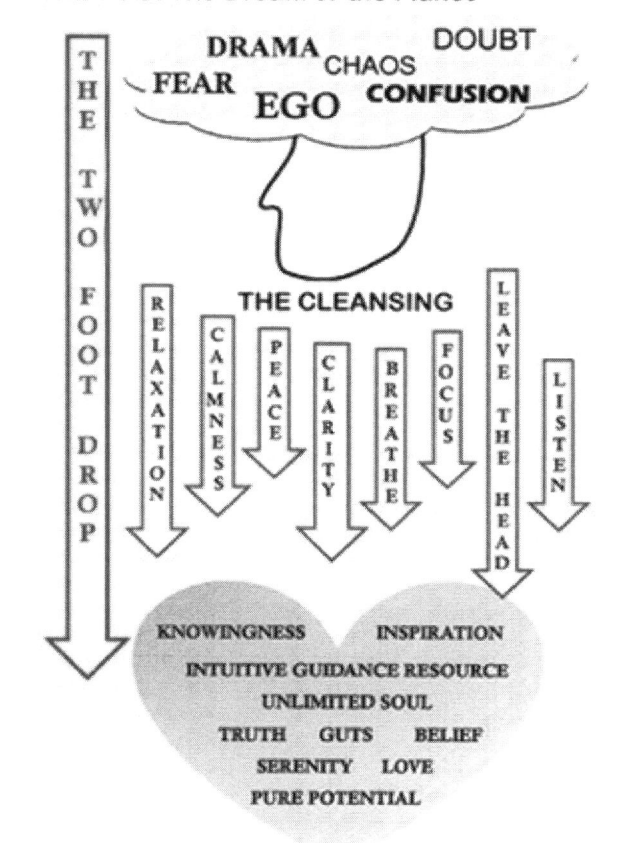

THE TWO FOOT DROP

DRAMA CHAOS DOUBT
FEAR EGO CONFUSION

THE CLEANSING

RELAXATION | CALMNESS | PEACE | CLARITY | BREATHE | FOCUS | LEAVE THE HEAD | LISTEN

KNOWINGNESS   INSPIRATION
INTUITIVE GUIDANCE RESOURCE
UNLIMITED SOUL
TRUTH   GUTS   BELIEF
SERENITY   LOVE
PURE POTENTIAL

CHAPTER 5

THE HEAD WE CHOOSE TO LIVE IN AND THE HEART WE LEFT BEHIND

We have been given the most efficient data processing computer known to man – our brain. It's up to us to see the beauty in this powerful machine with which we are all equipped. Like a computer it picks up viruses and installs defaults. These defaults I choose to call memory associations and have also been referred to as peptides or neuro-associations. This forms our personal and unique blueprint that is layered with our equally unique and individual life experiences. Most important, this thing we call the brain received its programming in our early years, and never really stops programming or loses its programming capabilities. This would explain why some people continue to grow and learn all their lives. Likewise there are people who, at some point in their life, made a conscious or sub-conscious decision not to continue personal growth for one reason or another. Generally some sort of emotional, financial or physical pain has to happen for the average adult to choose to grow, or at least reach out for something that might help them. A lot of us reach out when the going gets really tough, and then withdraw our extended hand immediately upon feeling better. This is what I call *Band-Aid behavior.* Have you ever had someone close to you behave in this way? They are always at the edge, and clearly in need of moral support or positive encouragement. We give it to them in hopes that they will grab hold of some tools and overcome their constant emotional, financial or mental limitations. When they don't grab hold, you end up saying *"do you want me to just listen or do you want my help?"* I have had many relationships like this. I discovered these relationship choices stemmed from my relationship with my mom. When I was a kid, I was trained to be the *fixer.* I formed an early association to fixing problems because my mom was severely out of control, trying to find herself through alcohol or whatever mind altering means possible. I was a bright loving kid with positive solutions even at the young age of 11 years old as I mentioned earlier. Through my own personal growth I have been able to back track and see why I have chosen these fixing types of relationships. In all of my problem relationships I can clearly see now what role they played and what role I was most definitely playing out "again." *(Is this one my mom or my dad? And so on and so forth?)* This pattern of choices will continue all the way through life unless we awaken. My choice pattern and knowledge of relationships has led me to choose so much chaos in my life just because I did not know any better. I want to be clear on how I feel today. **I am absolutely certain that I chose this life, all of it.** I knew it was exactly what I needed to become the person that I am today. Today I can see, much quicker and with more clarity, the proverbial anchors on the ships where relationships are concerned. When it comes to my professional relationships, I saw the endless rabbit hole of energy in my choices with the people in which I came into contact. Having been self-employed consistently for 10 years as a land developer, I have literally gone through the wringer of pain, turmoil, and abuse from my inability to choose the right people with which to do business. The right choices are so vital for any level of success, but especially in business. I have believed for some time that you have to give it away to keep it. I also felt this way about my livelihood/business by giving opportunities to others. For me, I loved that it offered endless channels for my creativity in finding, developing, financing, and ultimately selling it. It was mentally stimulating and I loved what I did. Even when the current economic situations made it hard in real estate, I still loved it. Over the years, I have had people around me that have been curious about what I do. So I pushed and convinced them to learn what I know because it was obvious to me it could enhance their life. I have always been the kind of person that if I find a good thing in my life, I want to help others find it also, and thus pass it on. This is how my heart is. I always bulldozed past the fact that these people never once said *"Can you help me?"* and I went on to push things on them because *I* could see they could clearly use the opportunity. *(Here comes the fixer -Ta-daa!)* Wow! The chaos I created combined with premeditated resentment based on my expectations that they would ultimately appreciate me, was astounding. What a mess. I enabled people to the point where they just expected things from me, leaving no room for a real respect or appreciation of me at all. Blindly I was ultimately robbing people of that experience of growth not to mention myself as well.

My journey in personal growth gave me the tools to take an appraisal or inventory of myself, leading me to realize that I was continuously acting as the giver in relationships. I could clearly see my motive reflected in the choices I was making. Because I found this to be such a valuable tool, later on in this book I will outline the steps necessary for you to do a self-assessment of your relationships. I promise it will be nothing short of enlightening if not totally liberating at the same time. In my case, by doing the things I was doing *(the fixing or the giving)* I would be loved or acknowledged as the good person I really am *(my ideal relationship with Mom)*, ultimately gaining the acknowledgment I never had growing up. My past relationships have been all about this sort of thing. I once heard it said that we pick our partners to process our childhood. Well that certainly applied to me.

The Epiphany

One night when I had friends over, my epiphany, or "ah-ha" moment if you will, came when I was nearing the end of a three-year relationship. As the evening was ending, I was standing in my hallway talking with a good friend about what was going on at that time in my life. In retrospect, I was venting more than anything, trying to sort through the confusion and frustration I was having in my current relationship. The hallway light was on in the background as we were talking, and I was leaning against the wall with my left shoulder. I had just made the comment that sometimes I look at my girlfriend and I see my mom. This was an interesting thing to say because my girlfriend did not look like my mom at all. As that thought passed through my head, I remarked *"Funny, my mom didn't have blonde hair."* At that moment a picture hanging on the wall to my left caught my attention. The picture, probably taken between 1965 and 1967, was of my mom, dad, grandmother and my older brother and I. In this picture my mother had the same color hair as my girlfriend, blonde! My epiphany was that I was in a relationship that mirrored the one I was in as the 5 year old boy in that photo.

Let me give you a bit more detail about the mechanics of the relationship between my mother and father. My mom and dad met when they around nineteen years old. They were very charismatic people and full of so much potential. They took a road trip to New Orleans where they both found work. My dad was modeling men's clothing and my mom got a job as a dancer at a mafia run night club. My father, a good looker, was a womanizer and it was not long until my mom caught him with another woman. Her knee jerk reaction to the devastation she felt at my dad's infidelity was to have a one night stand with the guy who ran the club where she was working. As a result of her infidelity, she became pregnant with my brother. My father accepted her pregnancy as the consequence for his wrong doings and, infidelities aside, they reconciled and stayed together to have my brother, and then me about 14 months later.

Here I was at 43 years of age in a relationship that had the same mechanics as the relationship my mother and father brought me into. In my girlfriend's case, the relationship she had with the father of her second son was very similar. They met while she was pregnant with her first son. He accepted and raised her first son as his own and they had her second son while they were together. In the end it did not work out between them, but the similarities of her past in connection to mine were uncanny to me all the same.

The puzzle pieces inadvertently fell together for me looking at that picture with what felt like a new pair of eyes that night. For the first time, I realized all the similarities in past and present relationships centered on the desire I had my entire life, to *fix* my mom. My childhood had been cut short by having to deal with adult problems. That child who had been left behind was coming out in my adulthood. Ultimately, I was trying to fix a problem that had caused me emotional damage as a child. Up to that point, I had no idea this was what I was doing. My behavior and choices were propelled by a force I was unaware existed within me. I was choosing emotionally unavailable women as partners.

Unknowingly, I was choosing partners that did not know how to accept and express the love for me that I longed for my whole life. I was unintentionally choosing this just wishing, hoping and waiting for the acknowledgement FINALLY that I am a beautiful, thoughtful loving person, the Epiphany. It is very important for me to stress that all of the women from my past are, and were, beautiful spirits and children of God, each on their own individual journey. This book is all about *Self* – it is all about the journey within, taking the time for self-appraisal, or seeking the "why," and growing with the answer.

The very act of slowing down *(for maybe 30 days or so)* just to get to know ourselves, is so honoring. We are each worth the time it takes to get to know ourselves, our story and our individuality. From this we are able to identify the cause and effect we have experienced in every relationship we have had. Most importantly, from this we can begin to create the greatest love story ever told – our own!

CHAPTER 6

UNCOVER, DISCOVER AND RECOVER
"When We Are At The Edge Of The Cliff The View Is So Clear."
~~~~~~

When did we become the executioner of our dreams, our happy endings and, most importantly, how did we become jaded?

I would like to describe what *uncover, discover and recover* means to me. Life has the uncanny ability of covering up these realities, true feelings and parts of our character in such a way that we are unaware they exist. When we discover these realities, feelings and parts of our character the possibility for change reveals itself to us. At this point, what we do with what is revealed is the key. Do we stuff our reality away, or are we finally ready to recover with new information and tools? When we look closely at the true meaning of our three objectives here, it becomes a little easier to accomplish our goal. *Uncover* represents the fact that we have things to find of which we were previously unaware. In this case I am referring to feelings, realities and parts of our character that, up to this point, remained hidden in the dark recesses of each of us. Discover shines the light into those recesses and brings these to the forefront in order for us to best deal with them. Recover is the grand finale in which we can use what we have learned about ourselves to grow and move forward in the bright and shining light of love of *Self* that we have obtained through this process.

As I mentioned before, other people can see through us at times creating awkward and uncomfortable situations. But in order to find these things, we need to be motivated to change. Unfortunately, most motivation comes from pain or loss on some level. However, we can have healthy motivation too. Inspiration, for example, is one form of healthy motivation to change. Whatever the motivating factor is, our main goal here is answering the question "How can I manifest the life I want today?" Here is where we choose to take some time off. The length of time is not as important as the quality and the follow through, to really dig in and have an awakening or life changing experience. Upon completion, the true success in this exercise comes in the clarity, peace and acknowledgement of a knowing and loving relationship with our *Self*. Not only are we worth it but so are the loved ones around us whom will also benefit from our experience.

Let us begin the journey with an exercise that will help you get a good look at cause and effect. Using a whole sheet of paper, separate it into four different columns and give yourself plenty of room to be thorough.

Column #1 – Who?

Your first column will contain the name of the person or entity at which you're angry or feel have been hurt by.

Column #2 – What?

Your second column is where you'll list in detail the event or exchange you experienced. What took place that has led you to feel the way you do today? Be specific. No matter how small the detail, if it affected you then, it matters today.

Column #3 – How?

Your third column is the "how." How were you affected? What feelings were ignited by this event? Again the need to be specific here is key. The more thorough you are, the more cleansing this process will be for you. To help pinpoint some of the common emotions there is a glossary at the back of this book for your reference and exploration. Often, in my personal journey it's been helpful for me to have a dictionary handy or some other book of reference to accurately and thoroughly identify my feelings in relation to events in my life.

Before we explore the fourth and final column I must say first and foremost, since you have completed the first three columns – welcome to freedom! The truth *will* set us free. Yes, as we have detailed, some people have wronged us. When those wrongs happened in our childhood or adolescence, we were truly powerless. But later on in our adult life, we have a choice. It is that freedom of choice that leads us to the fourth and final column.

Column #4 – My part

Your last column will only be difficult if you're not completely honest. The experience of seeing the cause and effect of our actions spelled out in front of us in black and white can be a myriad of things for us. In this column, we detail our part in the whole situation. Deep down we all recognize our contribution to the things that happen to us, good and bad. This is the place to transfer that recognition and, once and for all, deal with it head on. This is where we begin to see our responsibility in the course our life has taken up until now.

You now have the freedom of the power that comes from

the ability to see your side in all that happens in your life. You now hold the greatest gift one could ever have in a lifetime – *Self-awareness*. You can now clearly see where you may have to have a meeting with someone dear or that once was dear to you. You will now know what to say. You will now be clear and specific, which is very important in making an amends like this. Once I have reached this point in the past, what has worked best for me is calling someone up and saying to them *"I've been thinking a lot about the past and I would like to know if we could meet for coffee?"* Then if given the opportunity for this meeting, it is then important for you to be totally direct with them. It is important that you are careful not to set it up for them to feel sorry for you. When done correctly, you might be very surprised of what generally happens with them after this experience.

For the process to be a success, all you have to do is keep an open heart. It is impossible and totally pointless to try and anticipate what their response will be, so it is important to keep your focus on your part. To begin you could say something like "I regret that when I…. *(followed by the action or words you regret)*. Then allow them to express their feelings, being careful not to interrupt or take away their feelings. The key is humility in this experience. Once you are confident they have shared their feelings, it is important that you then you come up with a game plan to repay or do whatever is needed to rectify the original wrong actions or words. And make sure you follow through with your agreement to this person. Once this meeting is complete your side is now clean. If you have got more on your list you are now free to move on to the next person.

Here is a sample self-help tool for Self-awareness

Based on the hypothetical situation of my resentments with Nancy, my boss at a former place of employment.

FIRST COLUMN	SECOND COLUMN	THIRD COLUMN	FOURTH COLUMN
Person, place or thing	What happened	Effects my...	My part
Nancy	My boss, was always mean, rude, minimizing	Self-esteem, security, anger, pride	Chose to work there. Did not leave when maybe I should have

On this chart, based on the answers in the second column, the conclusion that my anger at Nancy is justified seems on track, right? She's rude to me, minimizing and always mean. My anger could further be justifiable because I had to make money to support my family at the time, and this was the best job I could find in the current job market with my qualifications, and "STOP"! I chose to work there, plain and simple. That it was all I could find at the time based on my qualifications could stem from my choices, years before, not to seek higher education or training. The point is, I precipitated the occurrences that led to my employment, wherein I worked for a difficult person. My objective is to get out of the victim role and stop playing the blame game. Choices and relationships require full ownership on our part in every aspect of our lives.

Sample chart for personal relationships
Based on my hypothetical relationship with Cindy that was fast moving and ended in betrayal.

FIRST COLUMN	**SECOND COLUMN**	**THIRD COLUMN**	**FOURTH COLUMN**
Person, place or thing	What happened	Effects my...	My part
Cindy	Betrayal	Security, Self-esteem, pride and anger	I saw evidence of her prior life with lots of relocating. I did not move with caution. I went quick – I fell in love with the good things and ignored the red flags

In this second example, again it is easy for us to justify and not see our side in the experience. *By the way my definition of "justify" is 'Just-If-I'.* But the "my part" column again details exactly what part I played when I am completely honest. It was my choice to overlook those red flags. I fell in love quickly and ignored the opportunity to make a responsible decision based on what I knew about this persona from the very beginning. We live in a world that believes that two wrongs make a right. Do unto others as they do unto you. In reality, the latter is misquoted to serve the intended purpose. The true quote is *"Do unto others as you would have them do unto you."* Again, our lack of honesty ends up giving us mixed messages.

I had a similar resentment in a long term relationship in my life. The scope of the resentment was that my partner was not willing to grow and communicate. I was miserable and felt alone most of the relationship. As a result, I would react and do things that were not healthy. Finally, I reached the point where I had to ask for a separation. When I completed my house cleaning on the whole situation, I wanted to make amends in great detail of the various things I did over the course of this long term relationship. It was suggested to me that the amends should be my regret that when things were not workable between the two of us and that I lacked the integrity and honesty to leave the relationship when I should have. After more thought I realized how 'right on' this simple suggestion was, and I realized that was the root of the problem that caused all of the chaos. In the end my amends were simple. I regretted that I lacked integrity and honesty in the relationship.

I share my personal experience on this subject to express the irony with which so many of us can relate. We remain in unhealthy relationships way too long, because we feel victimized in some way. In that, a vendetta towards the other person is born. This happens all too often and as society evolves, there is a growing number of people feeling personally victimized. One sad example of this was the story of the husband from Modesto, California whose pregnant wife disappeared. Subsequently his girlfriend and the body of his pregnant wife surfaced in that order thus exposing the sordid details of how one man chose a violent extreme solution to his inability to be honest with everyone involved. He lacked simple integrity and honesty, and in that could not end the relationship with his wife and admit that he wanted out of their relationship. On the outside and to all their friends and relatives they seemed to be a match made in heaven, but no one knew the double life he had chosen to lead. This is an extreme example, but the end result was the senseless deaths of two innocent people: his unborn son and his wife, all over not being happy in a relationship and the inability to be honest.

We hallucinate and become prisoners without even realizing that we chose this life. But on the other hand there are great stories of awakening and making a stand for love and respect of *Self* and therefore others. Tina Turner is a great example when she chose to end an abusive relationship, and walked out with only the clothes on her back. No pun intended, but Tina found her voice, and it is our voice and our choice that sets us free. None of us are victims when it comes to these specific situations with our choices and relationships.

The Law of Attraction

How do we make a clean break from our past, to our present, and therefore create our future? As I reflect back today on my business affairs and relationships, there were a lot of bad choices and lessons for me. Hindsight is 20/20, and after clarity and growth I now see the difference. Being the expressive person that I am, I have always carried a sense of testimony to help others at times or just maybe to confirm things in my life. I was completely baffled that, after knowing what my mistakes and bad choices were, for the next two years it got even worse for me with business. I did not know that I was recreating this in my life by continuing to share so much of what I did not want to happen to me anymore. That sharing kept me still living and choosing it. What I know today is by talking about what I did not want; I kept attracting it into my life. This was utterly confusing for me. Rehashing the same bad scenarios over and over again will keep us living in them over and over again simply because of the law of attraction, like attracts like. We need to identify what it is we do not want and then let it go.

The New Dream: Love and Happiness

Now that we have identified what we do not want to happen, that has been filling up empty space and resonating in our deepest thoughts, we can begin to replace and fill up that space with what we do want.

Try this: Write out exactly everything you do want and keep it with you so you can read it whenever you have the opportunity. Read it at night before bed, in the morning before beginning your day, whenever. The idea is that by doing this, you will affirm what it is that you want by owning it and claiming it as yours. What we do not realize is that by merely dreaming about what it is that we want we are creating the separation from those things, or continued want. When we claim they are already ours, we are no longer (wanting) separated from them.

Here I was thinking that I was coming from a place of compassion by sharing my growth and life lessons with others. In essence, although I learned the "wisdom to know the difference", I was not letting it go. At that time it felt like I were the communicator and being helpful to others. Today, this can help others in this book that, like me, did not know any better. During those following two years I continued through despair and turmoil that will hopefully save another. This has been the mantra in my life: "Why does this keep happening?"

Fear and the Law of Attraction: Pick a Dream

We can create what we fear in our lives by continuing to talk about it or continuing to allow the fear inside. We can be deceived because our head can truly know the difference and know what we do not want, but our deepest thoughts can still be talking to us or resonating within us, therefore still living and creating.

Purpose of Amends

This book's ultimate mission is "we want to be set free". When taking time off for ourselves and doing such a thing as this personal housecleaning the truth will set us free when we are willing to look at our side of our life path, journey. The amends process ends up giving us more benefits than anyone else ultimately, in our personal amends experience. My personal amends experiences have ranged from a person replying to me stating "I really forgot all about it", and to also opening up floodgates of another person's emotions, meaning they did not know how to do something like this until I called forth our meeting. I assure you when I say the truth will set you free you will walk 1,000 pounds lighter. Sometimes we just don't know the load we are carrying until we let it go. Now this moves us to forgiveness of others and most important, ourselves which I will share more on in the final chapter of this book which is entitled YOU the final chapter forgiveness.

A New Life Awaits You

We can become whoever we want to be in this lifetime. We can start over at any time. We can clean away and change our wrongs to rights. At any time you feel it is necessary, you can sit down with a sheet of paper and complete the columns we went through in the previous section. This exercise is helpful with any situation you encounter in your life that gives you trouble. We are totally in control of what happens in our lives if we are consistently aware of the part we play in the situations that arise.

Remember that we are ultimately powerless over other people in how they react or feel. All that is needed for our true happiness is inside us. As long as we know in our heart that we have shown up and taken the right, loving action, we are free, happy and truly joyous.

CHAPTER 7

RELATIONSHIPS/CHOICES
~~~~~~

"You're the smallest brightest light in the center of it all, as it unfolds, as it should. You can wait or you can choose to begin." *(Song lyrics I wrote)*

We can manifest the relationships we truly desire in this lifetime. Now that you have taken the time to become clear and to awaken your heart and your head, you are armed with the greatest gift you could ever give yourself: Self-knowledge. Now that you were able to identify some key elements, such as fear, doubt and love, you can live in the new perception that the past does not equal the present or the future. You can continue to grow now that you have some tools and some clarity, and can take inventory of yourself as you go from here. All too often we have an awakening from a book and then never look at it again. We can listen to our heart. We can listen to our head. Most importantly, we *can* learn how to see clearly and stay open to receive all the bliss that true love has to offer. Armed with the fact that deep down we are all beautiful, innocent and vulnerable children inside, we can become un-jaded.

Be Smart with the Heart

In choosing a life partner, slow down. What's the rush? We do not need to be on a crazy train any longer. We already know it takes at least four to six months, sometimes longer to get to know a person. However, the real key is getting to know yourself as best you can first. In doing so, not only will you be clearer about what you want out of a relationship, you will be able to give more to the relationship as well.

With our head clear from senseless chatter, we can be more likely to hear (listen) to our guidance intuition which can be a powerful "love train." I find it amazing that there is not a class or study group, at least in high school, that can touch on some of these crucial elements pertaining to relationships, even as simple as friendships. Because of the lack of education where relationships are concerned, many kids without one or both parental figures wind up struggling with relationships in adulthood, and inevitably learn by trial and error *(just like me)*. Some people get it soon, some later. Unfortunately, some never get "it" so they are unable to provide an example of a good and healthy relationship, as was my parent's case. Whatever the case may be, I believe it (love) is the truest and most divine experience we long for whether we know it or not.

Co-dependency

I wanted to touch lightly on this subject between these covers as I am personally co-dependent. I have been more than just "aware" of it, but have been working on it the last twenty years of my life. I like to say I was seasoned in co-dependency growing up. I grew up with the drama of an alcoholic family. I was trained at an early age to protect either my mom or my brother.

My perception of a relationship was to take care of, and try to fix, everyone around me. It was my purpose, or so I thought. My tendency with my choices was to find someone who needed to know what real love and sincerity were. I now know who I was, and the real reason I would choose these projects. It's because all along - *I was the project.* As I mentioned earlier, I kept choosing women who were like my mom and trying to fix them *(ultimately translating to fixing my mom).* There is a lot of co-dependency out there. Some people are aware of it and some are not. I have, and continue to process, this awareness so much in my life that

I have actually made light of the situation at some of my music shows. In between songs I have played a character with the first name of Cody and last name of Pendent. After I introduce myself everyone says "Hi, codependent" and I then play out a silly role of a co-dependent guy. Interestingly enough, some people laugh and others look offended or violated in some way. While my heart's purpose is never to hurt anyone, I have realized that some people have processed this subject and some people have not. In either case, there is a lot of it going around. There are many helpful books to shed light on this subject. One author that I've found to have extensive depth on this subject is Melody Beattie. I have found her books very helpful on this subject as I uncover, discover and recover in my life.

Individuality

We are completely responsible for robbing ourselves of our individuality. If we have a firm grasp of our own identity no one can take away our individuality without us letting them. When we do not take the time to have a relationship with ourselves, we might find there is quite a bit of confusion at the beginning of any relationship we enter. Knowing where they (the other person in the relationship) end and where you begin can be quite difficult without adequate self-knowledge and learning to coexist can be challenging in this situation.

We actually can learn how to agree to disagree and still be partners. However, if we have been raised in an environment where we were minimized, we could still be looking to others for that acknowledgement so that we can be affirmed about our individual belief. When all along it is us and our own self-esteem and belief in ourselves for which we are searching. Coming from that background it's so hard for us to truly live and let live. A few years back, my two boys were fighting in the backseat of the car. One was telling me a story and the other kept interrupting him. Finally, I stepped in and said "Let your brother have his story and don't take it away from him." To which he replied "Brilliant! Ok, but when he's done can I take his story away from him?" *Wow!* I thought.

My trials and errors are what inspired this book and are what made me realize one of the number one purposes in my life - the ability to make an impact in another person's life. Through trial and error, amazing depths of death, sorrow and heartache in my own life, I realized that nothing, absolutely nothing happens by mistake. As long as we keep going and seek our own individual purpose this is the great adventure of life – the why and the purpose. My greatest heart's desire is for others to take this journey. Yesterday is history and tomorrow is a mystery. If I did not lack love and relationships so much as a child, I would not have searched so much to find out the true meaning of it all.

A Look at the Four Elements of a Successful Relationship

Some time ago I had a vision of a relationship. The more I shared it and talked about it, it became clearer for me. What I envisioned was a table with four legs, each of which represented an element of a healthy relationship. Those elements are communication and respect representing the first two and honesty and listening representing the third and fourth elements.

Let's take a look at this and see if we have a tilted table or it could have half of it on the ground, in some cases the whole table might be missing legs.

Relationship table

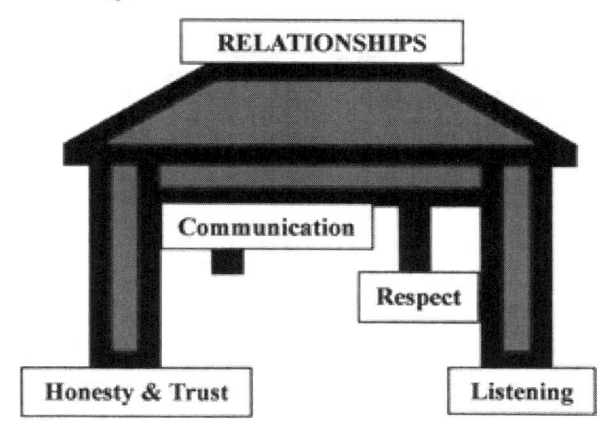

RELATIONSHIPS — Communication, Respect, Honesty & Trust, Listening

Communication

Are we getting angry because our partner should know how we feel, or are we willing to express how we feel with patience and love? All of this works both ways and it is important that we have someone in our life who wants to hear how we feel and what we have to say. A lot of times we think we are clear when sometimes we're not. In essence we know what we mean, but will the other person get our intended meaning? Learning how to do this is vital and number one; it's the roadmap to everything. The more you have communicated with yourself *(Self-awareness)* the more you can communicate effectively with another. We tend to get caught up in thinking that our feelings are not important or that our feelings don't matter. This only winds up manifesting its way out sideways with mixed messages inevitably only leading to more confusion. Nothing in life is more frustrating than someone being angry with you, and you not having a clue as to why they are angry. In life, at the end of the day, everything matters when it comes to the heart.

Honesty and trust

Let's face it; at the beginning of every relationship we enter into we are on our best behavior, right? Inadvertently dishonest, we just don't realize sometimes that in the long run there is less pain in being honest in the beginning of a relationship, than the pain we will face in four to six months later when we explode from holding in our truth. We need to be real. In essence we are people pleasing and do not want to rock the boat. This does not work. Honesty is essential in every relationship, yet there are many people playing this game on a regular basis. Aligned with communication, honesty is the highway used to express how you feel. I have experienced someone in my life being an honest person, but not possessing the ability to be honest with themselves. Just another example of denial, I spoke of this throughout this book. Self-honesty is self-awareness.

Earlier in this book I made the statement of how awkward it can be to know someone more than they know themselves. In most situations like this conflict is almost for sure. It is important that we do our part in a relationship and take our own inventory. All too often we demand so much without being willing to give what we want to get. This is where our ego kicks into overdrive. Ultimately it all comes down to asking ourselves "do we want to be right or do we want to be happy?" I am not saying that your truth is not important. I am saying that if your truth is questioned in a loving communicative way, we need to be open to another's truths and willing to grow. Openness and honesty are the two best words you can focus on in your quest for manifesting the relationship you want today. To help in manifesting a shift, write these words on post-its and keep them highly visible. Openness and honesty are where the peace lies and where we cease fighting others. Our most damaging thought, or hallucination if you will, is thinking that if the other person knew the truth about us, they would run *(fear of abandonment)*. Truth is real love is more substantial than that.

Respect

Here's something that we can agree upon that is important for all of us, yet seems so lost in the world today: respect. I think respect is one of the greatest things we can teach our kids on a daily basis. If we can instill the true meaning of the word in our children, we would be doing our part in changing the world. Respect is defined as the act of considering worthy of esteem. I think the lack of this priority is easily missed in today's society. So many of us that are adults now, never got it growing up and it shows in today's disregard for human life. We all really need to keep the true meaning of this word at the front of our minds and understand the depth of it. In just one day's time the lack of respect in the world can be so violating. For some people just to be rude and minimize others and have a lack of regard for humanity there is no reason other than it's a way of life. Yes, there is a reason everybody is struggling with their own insecurities of feeling less than others. A lot of people feel the need to bring you down. A while back I thought of creating a short film about a day in the life of a man who is dreading going out into the world. We can feel so run over even in a couple of stops at customer service counter for example. I realized however that it had already been made into a movie starring Michael Douglas called *Falling Down*.

Take a look at respect as a key element in a relationship. It can be described as acknowledgement, regard for that person enough to be honest with them and to communicate that concern for their humanity with your honesty. I believe if a person conducts themselves with a high level of respect in their daily life they will be a person of integrity who may do what they say and say what they do. In this we obtain self-esteem, and again we're back to a relationship with *Self*. You must have self-respect to obtain respect. Be it, get it.

A friend of mine shared a story about his wife and how she had quite a bit of frustration with his way of doing things. She told her sponsor all about it. To indulge her obvious frustration, her sponsor said ok and, with what seemed a great interest to help, told her to write down all the things she wanted her husband to be. When this was done, she was to call her sponsor back and they'd meet and go over a game plan on how to fix these things. My friend's wife, excited at the prospect of having the opportunity and support with somebody who was finally on her side, made a long list. When the day came she brought her long list to the coffee house to meet with her sponsor and with excitement passed the list across the table to her sponsor. Her sponsor passed the list back across the table and said "Great, now you be all those things." Talk about bursting a bubble! The point of this is that if you want love, give love. If you want a friend, be a friend. If you want respect, give respect.

Listening - The act of listening is compassion and understanding.

Listening puts respect and communication into play. It is in the act of listening that we are giving respect and regard to others. The other half of communication is listening. Of course, I had run into issues with this a lot. Unbeknownst to my partner, I am in deep thought on something all the while looking at her while she is talking to me. It totally looks like I am listening to her but I know I am only going through the motions. She does not know this unless I say "sorry I was deep in thought, let me focus now," which are the times when I have not heard her. I try to pay attention to that today and realize that no matter how many times I think I can multitask, when it comes to listening, if I am multitasking inevitably I would miss something. I have had to learn about the importance of listening, especially when it comes to matters of the heart. We can hear, but are we really listening? How many of us can relate to this from personal experience? Maybe we have regret over a past relationship that with hindsight, we can clearly see how our partner was trying to get across things that were very vital to the moment and we disregarded the importance of them. We all need to feel heard especially by our significant others. If they are our true life partners, they are also our allies and best friends. Therefore, we need to make them matter because being all of those things to us, they too are worth it just as much as we are. I can't stress it enough; if you want to be heard, listen.

Intimacy: *Into-me-I-see*

We can all experience intimacy no matter what your path has been, such as mine. Intimacy is there for all of us. I think that a lot of us can be ten miles in the woods on this, and some of us hundreds of miles in the woods. In other words, we are in the woods equally – some more so, some less. We can all obtain it if we can identify the need for it and if it is something we truly desire in this lifetime. Again, as long as we are willing, *all the answers lie in seeing inside ourselves.* The only one we're usually running from is ourselves. I invite you to take this journey – this voyage in this lifetime. Experience all the riches that true success can bring a true love story………. you.

Continuity: *Continuing – unity*

A lot of us have a negative association to the thought that a relationship takes work. My own association to the term was that it was a ton of work, because all of the relationships I chose were more projects than anything else. They also served as a diversion at the time from the project I did not want to take on – myself. Ultimately, once we can become clear on what is ours and what is not, the work becomes less. We can then possibly have a new association to the term "a relationship requires work." A relationship requires a desire and the motivation to have one. A simple willingness is necessary to be open, honest and grow, especially when both people are coming from severely dysfunctional families. We can have a daily reprieve from a dysfunctional relationship if we choose. This is where the term it takes two to have a relationship came from. In the meantime and for all time, you can have a successful relationship with yourself by continuous unity with yourself. Use these tools as a life practice as you go on from here. "We get what we settle for." The choices are all yours. You are no longer a victim. We are not trapped. We are not prisoners.

CHAPTER 8

YOU: THE FINAL CHAPTER, FORGIVENESS

Even if we seem to think there is some level or classification for forgiveness in situations, there is not. Even for people who have badly scorned us and done things we, as humans, feel are unforgivable, it is quite the contrary. They are even more deserving of forgiveness. We have the illusion that forgiveness is something we are humbly doing for someone else, but when we forgive it is for us equally and maybe even more so. The very process of forgiving another human being is vital for our freedom and for our souls to be free. Forgiving enables us to be free. Resentment is poison, it can eat you alive.

Most of all, from that inventory process we took in the exercise of this book, what I would like to call a house cleaning, we must first forgive ourselves. This is the pillar to which we reconnect, like a long lost love to ourselves; the *Self* with which we have really been missing up until now. Sit down in a quiet, loving union with yourself and go through all your trials and errors. You must have this experience to forgive yourself, for you are a spiritual being having a human experience. Forgive yourself just for the fact that you truly did not know any better – and now you do.

You have shown up for yourself and taken the time for a relationship with yourself. You are the most important person on this planet now. You now have the light, the tools to process things at any given time. You have the wisdom to know the difference and now you can embark on the greatest love story ever told – YOURS!

Love, Love, Love
Lance T. Painter

GLOSSARY OF WORDS/FEELINGS

Fear	to be afraid of; apprehension, anxiety, solitude, alarm, dread, panic, dismay, terror
Lust	desire, ache for; yearning, hunger, thirst
Envy	a feeling of discontent and ill will at another's excellence or good fortune; jealousy
Possessive	the act of having or taking into control or occupancy of property of someone without regard to ownership demanding exclusivity; wishing to control somebody exclusively or to the sole object of somebody's love
Covetous	an implication of selfishness and often suggests unfair or ruthless means to want somebody else's property
Pride	excessive self-esteem, conceit, arrogance
Lazy	unwilling to do any work or make an effort; indolent
Greed	an overwhelming desire to have more of something than is actually needed, such as money
Security	the state or feeling of being safe and protected, the assurance that something of value will not be taken away; safety
Faithful	consistently trustworthy and loyal, believing firmly in something or somebody; loyal, devoted, trustworthy, committed

Sincerity — honesty in the expression of true or deep feelings; genuineness, honesty, earnestness, authenticity

We can manifest the relationships we truly desire in this lifetime. We can listen to our heart. We can listen to our head. And we can have the wisdom to know the difference.

Lance T. Painter ~ 2013

13554700R00057

Made in the USA
San Bernardino, CA
26 July 2014